Soulful
REFLECTIONS

Linda L Franklin

AuthorHouse™
1663 Liberty Drive
Bloomington, IN 47403
www.authorhouse.com
Phone: 833-262-8899

This book is printed on acid-free paper.

ISBN: 978-1-6655-6366-6 (sc)
ISBN: 978-1-6655-6365-9 (e)

Library of Congress Control Number: 2022911827

Print information available on the last page.

Published by AuthorHouse 12/09/2022

authorHOUSE®

CONTENTS

DEDICATION

Soulful Reflections has been in the making since I first started writing poetry in 2007. Some of these poems may be about certain people, but most of them are about the essence of a soul either in this life or in past lives that my soul identifies with and continues to search for in this life. These poems are also inspired by the women in my life that have contributed to my growth in some way, or just by giving me unconditional love and encouragement. I want to personally thank some of the many wonderful women who have inspired me. They are listed in no particular order, as I really do not have room to list everyone, so I am just going to mention a few. A special thank you to Patricia Vierling, Megan Guthrie, Sue Pearce, Terri Cuseo, Jerri Haines, Marla Adams, Mary Magill Orysiek, Brenda Currier, Joy Wilson, Beverly Sobieski, Wanda Rodrequze, Rebecca Tucker Cecil and Jean Howard. You ladies are amazing and will always hold a special place in my heart. Each and every one of you are an inspiration and I love you all beyond words.

A BEAUTIFUL SOUL

When I first looked into your eyes, I saw
Your beautiful soul and it touched my heart.
I saw a soul that has fought battles
A soul that has known love and lost it
A soul that has weathered storms and survived
A soul that has had to endure the heartaches of being on earth.

God has counted his angels and discovered one was missing
And when I look into your eyes, I see that soul
You should not be here, But I'm glad you came.
When I look at you, your soul soothes mine.
I feel your soul surround me and encase me in your light and love.
With all the pain you have endured
Your light shines forever more.
And you did it all because you have a beautiful soul.

A FRIEND

A friend is there even when you can't see them.
A friend is there even when you can't touch them.
A friend is there even when you are miles apart.
A friend is there like the breeze upon your hair.
A friend is there that brings a smile to your heart.
A friend is there, wrapping you in their love, even when you are alone.
A friend is there when you feel it in your heart.
You are my friend, and you are in my heart.

ALONE

Every day I'm with other people
Yet I'm alone
Maybe I'm in a crowded theater
A baseball stadium or a concert hall
Doesn't matter who is near
I'm alone.
There are times when I can feel you near me
Yet no one is around
Or I can hear you whisper in my ear
Words that no one can hear
You're in my thoughts
Whether I'm awake or asleep
As my travels take me around the globe
My mind and spirit are with you
Yet I'm alone
I walk city streets
And roam the countryside
Every day I'm with other people
Yet I'm alone.

ANCESTORS AND ME

My life just didn't start when I was born
It is interwoven with those who have come before.
Many people make up who I am
Some I have met, but for a few short years
Others have been gone long before I am.

From far-away lands they came to be
Looking for a better life for them and me
From all kinds of walks in life were they
But yet each has made an impact in some way

As my hair could be curly or straight
My eyes could be as dark as the night
Or as blue as the sky
My skin could be light or dark,
Or any shade in-between

My genes are what my ancestors gave to me
Whether it be shaping the country
Or shaping me
Their journey continues even in me.

Park Avenue in Arches
National Park, Utah

AS I LAY SLEEPING

As I lay sleeping
I feel your arms encircle me
As I stir in my sleep
our bodies are skin on skin.
My body is slowly starting to wake
as your fingertips gently
caresses my face and arms.
As I lay sleeping
I hear you whisper my name
While telling me how much
I mean to you
My body relaxes against yours
with the knowledge that
I am safe in your arms.
As I lay sleeping
I softly turn towards you
as you gently kiss my ear down to my neck
As I lay sleeping
You gently tell me to go back to sleep,
as you will be there in the morning light.

Walkway at Three Sisters ,
Crystal River, Fl.

AS I WALK

As I walk
The air is crisp and clear
The world is waking from its slumber
Early in the morning, as the sun
Is peeking over the horizon

As I walk
The air hasn't become heavy yet
with the sounds of traffic,
nor the movement of bodies
There is a stillness that surrounds me.

As I walk
My senses are alert
With the smells of mother earth
My ears are listening
To the silence of the forest

As I walk
My steps are strong,
My breathing is even
My body relaxed
My mind is clear

Where my thoughts
drift to you
As I walk.

Wild Bear cub in Keremeos, BC

BAD BECKY BAD

She looks very regal with her hair of red
And her blueish green eyes
A voice that drips southern style
But don't turn your back
Cause her tongue is sharp as ice
And she'll get you if she can
Bad Becky Bad
She must be from Ireland
Cause she's a little elf
In her green hat
And she has the gift of gab
Bad Becky Bad

Busy road in Vancouver,BC

CHANGES

Whether we want it to or not
It seems that things are forever changing.
Changes can be big, or they can be very small
Our thoughts change with the direction of the wind
Or so it seems.

Styles change from month to month,
Even our ideas change from day to day or year to year
What we once thought was so important
Is now something we can't even remember.

When we were young, we wouldn't eat some foods
But now we can't get enough of them
Even our sense of humor changes from time to time
What was once funny may now not be

Some friends may last a lifetime
While others for just a moment in time.
Some changes are thrust upon us
While others we make ourselves.

They say that nothing is permanent
But that I don't believe
Because no matter what changes
My love for you stays the same.

DON'T TELL ME

Don't tell me you love me,
Show me with your actions.
Don't tell me you are going to be there for me,
Then be gone when times get a little tough.
Don't tell me I am wrong,
when your actions show me, I am right.
Don't tell me things,
If you are just going to lie to me.
Don't tell me how you feel,
Show me your feelings, how you love.
Don't tell me you are a kind person,
Show me your kindness.
Don't tell me you are an honest person,
Show me your honestly.
Don't tell me how strong you are,
Show me your strength through your gentle and loving ways.
Don't tell me you love me,
SHOW ME.

Delicate Arch in Arches
National Park, Utah

DREAMS

A dream may start out small or big,
But no dream is too small or too big.

At times they may seem to be untouchable or unreachable,
But we all know that everything is touchable or reachable.

Dreams are what let's our hearts and souls fly,
So set your dreams free and watch them fly high.

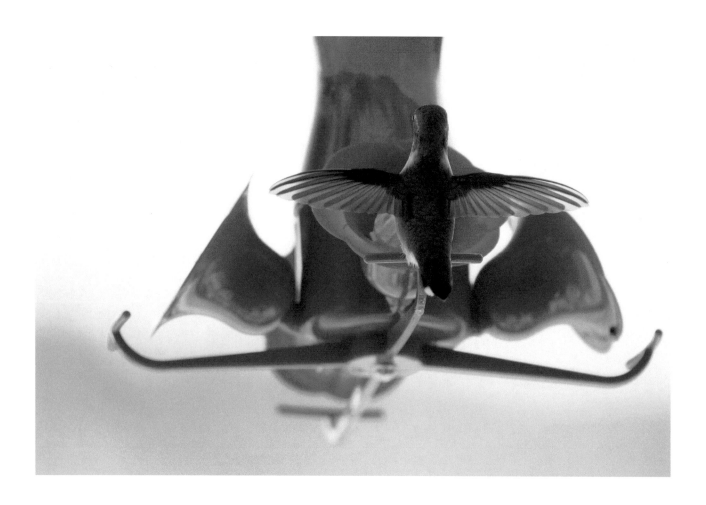

FREE SPIRIT

The waves beckon me to the shores
As the sun dances in the sky
The wind whispers my name
As it glides over the dunes
My soul cries for days of old
When my soul was young and free
A lifetime happens in a blink of an eye
And this life is over almost as soon as its begun
We were not together in this life
Our days are growing shorter
Soon we will be together at the shores
As the sun dances in the sky
We leave our footprints softly in the sand
The wind glides over the dunes
As our spirits become free again.

HE GREW TO BE LIGHTNING FAST

He was born to a family
Way to the north.
All he ever wanted to do
Was shoot a puck or two

He could skate better than he could walk
So, he practiced and practiced
As hard as he could,
Just so he could shoot a puck or two.

Into a fine young man he grew
At least 6' plus two
He played and played all through school
Just so he could shoot a puck or two

He grew to be lightning fast,
As his slap shot was 90 or more
And his team knew
He could shoot a puck or two

So, in the future, when you watch him play
Just know that he plays and plays
Just so he can shoot a puck or two
For you.

I AM

I was born into this world
As no one of importance except to a few
I grew and grew
Through living life's experience's
And learning from the ones around me
Many may not like me or understand me
As I do not do things to please others but me
I am an individual as:
I love who I want
I respect who I want
I trust who I want
And I listen to who I want,
But mostly I listen to me
Will I change the world?
Not that I believe
But if I'm lucky I may make a difference
To the people around me
Who Am I
Might you ask?
Just your friend
Is who I am

Orion's nebula 7,500 lightyears from earth.

I AM A TIME TRAVELER

My soul is eternal, it has no end
It has lived many lives in the past
And it will live many lives in the future
For I am a time traveler.

I have lived in many places on this world
Most I cannot remember
Except through my 6th sense and in my dreams
For I am a time traveler.

I have been a mother, daughter, father, son
Though out my many lives.
I have been cold, hot, indifferent, loving, caring, tolerant
For I am a time traveler.

I have loved many a soul and many a souls have loved me
Our love has no end and doesn't care who you are
Or the color of your skin. I will continue to love you
For I am a time traveler.

I have witnessed the world and have watched as it has changed
Through each generation that I have lived.
I have traveled all the seas and all the continents
And my journey is not done
For I am a time traveler.

I CARE

When you're upset
When you're down on your luck
Know that I care.

When you feel the world has turned its back on you
And you seem to have lost your way
Know that I care.

When you feel that you can't go on
When you are being pulled into too many directions
Know that I care.

When you need me to hold your hand,
Or lend a shoulder for you to lean on
Know that I am there
Because I care.

I KNEW YOU

I knew you when I first met you
I knew you just by looking into your eyes
Your eyes held my attention
Your smile would not let me go
I fell in love with you
Before you even spoke
We sat and talked for hours
Slowly our time was coming to an end
And I didn't want the afternoon to stop
Because I knew you and I would be apart again
Our lives just would not work in this life
My heart was breaking because I knew you
Fate was being cruel to us
We didn't even stand a chance
As much as we cared for each other
Forces were keeping us apart
No matter how hard we tried
We could not make it work
We had to say goodbye
But I am so glad I knew you.

Eagles Point state park in Iowa

I MISS YOU

I miss your smile
When you laughed how your eyes lit up
And the sound of your voice
I miss your humor
And your intelligent conversations
I miss You

I miss your gentle ways
How your touch would always calm me.
When I was hurt or upset
How you would reach for my hand
Just to let me know you loved me
I miss you

I miss your strengths
How you could easily handle
Any situation or occasion
I miss your logical mind
I miss you

I miss how we were one
When we were together
But most of all
I just miss you.

IF YOU LOVE ME

If you love me
Love me because I make you laugh
Love me because I make your heart skip a beat
whenever I am near you.
Love me because I bring a smile to
your face when you think of me.
Love me because I am like no others
that have come before.
Love me because you believe I am your soulmate.

If you love me
don't treat me like your previous loves
If you love me treat me as an equal
If you love me don't treat me as a China doll
If you love me be there for me every day.
If you love me don't gender play me

If you love me
don't expect me to act
like you think I should
If you love me
help me spread my wings and fly
If you love me, I want you to need me
If you love me,
you will do all of these
because you love me.

Northern Lights looking to the north from ,Keremeos, BC Canada

JUST A DREAM

Our eyes met across the room
You smile and my heart melts
My mind rushes – Who is this person
And where did they come from?
We danced, we laughed, we talked till dawn
Neither of us wanted the night to end
Because our life was just beginning
A slight memory stirs in my mind
My blood runs cold, I shiver
I awake just as a tear slides down my cheek
Because it was just a dream

Shuswap Lake, BC Canada

LOST

You came into this world with high expectations
But somewhere during your life it was lost
Your future was bright, but then your light was lost
You had big dreams and plans, but they were lost
Now we are lost because your life was taken from us.

LOVE HAS NO BOUNDARIES

So many times,
we think that Love can only survive
in the Boundaries that we have set for it;
But
Love doesn't care about hate.
Love doesn't care if you're wealthy or poor.
Love doesn't care to judge.
Love doesn't care whether you're healthy or sick.
Love doesn't care about beauty or scars.
Love doesn't care whether you're smart or not.
Love doesn't care about what color you are.
Love doesn't care what sex you are.
Love has no boundaries
Except the limitations that we set in our own minds.

LOVE WITHOUT

Love Without Respect is Nothing
Love Without Passion is Nothing
Love without Feelings is Nothing
Love without Compassion is Nothing
Love without Forgiveness is Nothing
Love without Trust is Nothing
Love without Honor is Nothing
Love without Laughter is Nothing
Love without You is Nothing
You are all of the above
and without you
I AM NOTHING

Stonehenge, England

ME AND THE POTS AND THE PANS

Just me and the pots and the pans
In my own little world
With my hands in the water,
My mind goes around the world
The peace, the quiet, the solitude
As my mind soars over France
We take journeys every day
Just me and the pots and the pans
To Italy, Spain, Morocco, Istanbul and Budapest
Dancing the night away in Rio
Or hitting the tables in Monaco
There's nary a place we don't travel
Just me and the pots and the pans.

Carb San Lucas, Mexico

MY HEART STILL REMEMBERS

You were my world
The light that made my soul smile
With you I felt so strong, so safe, so loved
Then you went away and took everything
But my heart still remembers,
Your touch, your smile, your voice, our souls as one
To you I'm just a distant mcmory
You have moved on to another life and love
I can't go back, nor can I move on because
My heart still remembers.

MY HEART WON'T FORGET

It's been a while since you were taken
At times the pain has been unbearable
The tears still flow freely and often
When I remember your laugh, the smile on your face
Our life together the way it was
My heart won't forget

You were taken from me before your time
We still had a thousand things to do
I wasn't ready to let you go
WE had dreams that died when you died
My heart won't forget

My life now has to go in another direction
Life is for the living and I'm just now
Starting to get on with my new life.
No matter where I go, what I do
Or who I meet
You will always be with me
In my heart, my mind, my soul
My heart won't forget

MY SOUL CRIES OUT FOR YOU

Through the years I have caught glimpses of you
At time I thought I had met you
You invade my dreams, my waking thoughts
My soul cries out for you

I know what kind of person you are: I know your kindness
Your strengths, your fears and what frightens you
As well as what you love
You and I are one - made of the same soul
My soul crics out for you

It should be easy to find you
But not knowing who you are or
What you look like, makes it hard.
Throughout our lifetimes I will never stop searching for you
Because my soul cries out for you

NOT BY BLOOD

In this journey of life
You are my sister
Genes do not bind us
Different mothers and fathers have we
We come from different
Parts of the world
But are united in our bond
You are my sister
Not by Blood, But by Love.

We may not see each other
As years may go by
But we are together
In heart and soul
You are my sister
Not by blood, but by love

My sister's may come
From different races
Some have deep religious roots
Others are spiritualist
And some are atheists
Doesn't matter we are one
You are my sister
Not by blood, but by love

We stand together because if
You hurt one
You hurt all of us
You mess with one
You mess with all of us
You are my sister
Not of by blood, but of my love.

NOT THE ONE FOR YOU

You say you want to be with me
You say you are in love with me
If I am not the one
You think about when you first wake up or
The last person before you go to sleep
Then I am not the one for you.

You say we belong together
But if I do not make your heart sing
Or put butterflies in your stomach
Or make your knees go weak when you see me
Then I am not the one for you.

If the thought of never seeing me again
doesn't break your heart
Or you don't want to spend your free time with me
Then I am not the one for you

If when you take me in your arms
And my kisses do not rock your
Soul to its core,
Nor does it make you want a life
Time of kisses with me
Then I am not the one for you

If you don't want to shower me with affection
and spoil me every chance you have, or
if you don't want to show me
how important I am to you everyday
Then I am not the one for you

For you see I would do all that for you.

PEACE TO THE SOUL

The waves gently lapping at my feet
As my worries leave my soul
No cars, no buses, no trains
The wind blows through the leaves
Making a song on the breeze

Birds scurrying on little feet
Looking for something to eat
Leaving imprints in the sand
As the waves gently lap
The shore at my feet

The sun plays peek-a-boo within the clouds
As pelicans skim over ocean's waves
With waves gently lapping at my feet
It's neither the fame nor the money
That brings peace to the soul
But the waves gently lapping at my feet.

REMEMBER ME

Remember me when I'm gone
Not with a heavy heart
Or sadness in your soul
But with a smile in your eyes
And Joy in your heart

Remember me when I'm gone
The times we laughed
The memories we made
Even the times we disagreed
They all make up you and me

Remember me when I'm gone
How we helped each other grow
How we learned from the mistakes
There's no time for sorrow or grief
When you remember me when I'm gone.

SECRET ADMIRER

When I saw you
Something stirred inside of me
We have never met
Yet I feel we should know each other.
I am drawn to you
For reasons I do not know
The pull is like a magnet
Your secret admirer
Chances of us meeting
Are slim to none
Our worlds are miles apart
Yet you are someone I should know
In my mind I imagine you and I
But know that it will not be
Just know there is someone
In this world that is thinking of you
Your secret admirer

Athabasca Falls, Alberta, Canada

SINCE I'VE MET YOU

For the first time in my life, I'm truly alive.
My Eyes are seeing everything in a new light.
I now know what direction my life lies.
You are the first person I think of when I awake,
and you are the last person I think of when I go to bed.
I am truly blessed by your love for me.
Your love amazes me.
I am no longer waiting for my true love –
You have arrived.
You are my teacher, my friend, my lover and my soul mate.
For all of the above,
I Thank-You and I Love you more than you will ever know.

SLEEP, SLEEP MY LOVE

Sleep, sleep my love
As the day has yet to break
You turn in your sleep
May your sleep bring you peace
May your sleep bring you happy dreams

Sleep, sleep my love
As the day has yet to break
You are mumbling in your sleep
As you lie there
I am watching over you
And you are safe from the world

Sleep, sleep my love
As the day has yet to break
All the troubles from days before
Have been put to rest
As you gently sleep, sleep my love.

SOMETIMES LOVE IS NOT ENOUGH

When we were young,
We believed in fairytales and happy endings.
Through the years we held on to believing
That love was always going to last.
When we met, I fell fast and hard for you,
You felt the same
For a time, we were so happy and in love
You were my world
But slowly the differences started pulling us apart,
We each saw it happening and we could feel the change
We tried but there was nothing we could do
Even though we are still in love,
It's so very sad when you realize that
Sometimes love is not enough.

STOLEN HEART

You stole my heart
Like a thief on the Nile
Our love, it has no boundaries
As it crosses borders and miles
Our love soars like a Hot Air Balloon
With your gentle ways and loving nature
Each day wc grow closcr as wc
Share our lives and become one
Your touch soothes my soul when it is troubled
And it all started on the Nile.

THE ONE THAT GOT AWAY

Have you ever wondered
About the one that got away
From so many years ago

Do you wonder
What your life would be like
Or where you would be living
With the one that got away

Would that person still look the same?
Or make you feel the way you did
With the one that got away

Oh, how the years have passed
Without the one that got away
You were so sure you couldn't live
Without the one that got away

Look at you now standing so tall
Being so strong, living so well
Ever wonder about the one that got away?
Yes, I am the one that got away.

TRUST

How do you learn to trust
When the one you loved betrayed you?
When all the trust has been destroyed
When the one you loved
No longer showed they cared
When the one you loved
Left you for another

How do you learn to trust
When someone says
They love you again
When someone wants
You to trust them
When someone wants you to commit to them

How do you learn to trust
Comes from your heart
Comes from the love shining in their eyes
Comes from the love you feel from them
Comes from the depth of your soul
Comes from believing
That it is meant to be.

UNMASK FOR ME

The world is looking for love
But love is masked on the faces of strangers.
When we were young – Love shown
Through every pore of our soul
Through our eyes, our smile, our touch, our face.
Through years of pain, broken hearts,
Lies and broken promises,
The mask slowly covered our soul
Where true feelings are rarely ever seen
To many times love is masked and
Really not seen
Then love slowly disappears
I want the love of the inner child
If you love me show me by the
Look on your facc,
the touch of your hand
The smile in your eyes
The excitement in your voice
The vibrations coming from your soul
I want the love from your inner child's love,
So sincere, so trusting, so vulnerable, so innocent
If you love me unmask your hurt,
Unmask your feelings,
Unmask your touch
If you love me,
Unmask for me.

WHEN ARE WE GOING TO LEARN?

Billions of people are abused in some way each and every day
When are we going to learn
That it's not ok to burn a child because they cry or wet their pants.
That saying hurtful or derogatory remarks leaves scars.
That it's not ok to hit when we're angry, hurt or things aren't going our way.
That people are not objects or possessions that we own.

When are we going to learn
That sex with a child is not ok, or
That sex without consent is a crime.
That loving a person of the same gender is not wrong, nor
Does it matter what color the skin is.
When are we going to learn
That people need our love, our support, our encouragement
Our acceptance.
When are we going to learn?

Delicate Arch in Arches National Park, Utah.

WHEN I LOOK AT YOU

Baby when I look at you,
I am in Awe.
You take my breathe away,
with the love I see in your face.
When you touch me,
An electrical shock runs through me.
When I look at you,
I see our future together
I see you and I
the way it should be, side by side.
Today, Tomorrow, Forever.
When I look at you,
I know that you are in love with me,
and will always be there for me.
When I look at You,
I see US
and my soul smiles,
because everything is now right with the world.
When I look at You,
I have now come home
and I will never leave you again.

Sunwapta Falls, Alberta, Canada

WHEN I'M NEAR YOU

My blood rushes to my head
My heart races and butterflies in my stomach try to get out
My hands shake and my body quivers
Thoughts make no sense
When I close my eyes, I can
Feel your lips on mine
My words get lost in my mouth
And fail to come out
This all happens
When I'm near you.

WHERE DOES LOVE GO?

Where does love go?
Once you tell someone you love them.
Once you've told them that they were your one and only.
And they were your soul mate for life.
All was right with the world.
You could do no wrong
Their touch sent electrical sparks through you
Then the next day, they won't even speak your name.
Where does Love go?
So fast in a blink of an eye?
Where does Love go?

WHO RULES

It's just a little thing
Only weighing 10 ounces or so
It has the power
To bring you to your knees
Or lift you up and let you soar.
It rules us
Whether we want it to or not
We can give it away
Or keep it close to us
It holds our most precious
Feelings and memories
Many will say
That it's the head that rules
But it is really the heart
Because wherever our heart is
Is where we are.

WILD ROSES IN THE BUSH

Wild Roses in the Bush
Wild Roses in the Bush
So soft, so sweet you are,

Wild Roses in the Bush
Wild Roses in the Bush
Climbing the heavenly vine,

Wild Roses in the Bush
Wild Roses in the Bush
Your Smell is worth the Thorns to Have You.
Wild Roses in the Bush.

YOU BROKE MY HEART

All of my life I had never really found someone to love
For years I had searched for you
My heart had never really loved before
No matter how hard I tried
No one could stir my feelings
You broke my heart

When we met, I was taken by surprise
At last, I had found you
Your eyes could hypnotize me
Your smile warmed my soul, and I was whole
You broke my heart

Years have gone since you left me
My heart aches all the time
My chest feels like it has a hole in it
And I know I'm not complete
You broke my heart

There are times when I rarely think of you
But then there are days you never leave my thoughts
At times I expect you to walk into the room and
At other times I never want to see you
You broke my heart

My heart is broken
And it will never heal
Would I ever take you back.......No
Because you broke my heart.

YOU'RE NOT THE PERSON
I THOUGHT YOU WERE

Months ago, I became attracted to you
I thought you had integrity,
Poise, charm and a kind heart
You seemed the perfect match for me
You're not the person I thought you were

You had me fooled from the beginning
With your caring manner and soft voice
You told me you were in love with me
And that I was your soulmate
You're not the person I thought you were

We never fought or disagreed
My feelings for you were growing stronger
And I couldn't wait till I saw you again
How was I to know you had another
And you were in their arms before we were though
You're not the person I thought you were

I just wonder how long before you get another..........

YOU'RE THERE

As I walk in this life
Taking the journey through time
You're there

Through all the times in life
I feel you
And know that I'm not alone
You're there

At times when I'm scared
At times when I'm lonely
At times I'm not sure where I'm going
You're there

Holding my hand
Wiping my tears
Soothing my brow
You're there

Speaking words of encouragement
Cheering me on
Believing in me
You're there

You never let me fall
As you always have my back
I'm so very glad
You're there

Vancouver, BC Canada

YOU WILL BE MISSED

You came into our lives
With your smiling face,
With your winning personality
You Will Be Missed

You Filled our Hearts with Joy
Always there to lend a Helping hand
You were the one everyone
Turned to when they needed advice
Or a shoulder to lean on.
You Will Be Missed

Now my friend, you must leave us,
Our hearts are heavy and sad
We will be lost without you
But know that you are loved and
You Will Be Missed

All photography in this book was photographed by Linda. L. Franklin, as well as the front and back cover.

*Following is an official **OnlineBookClub.org** review of "Soulful Reflections" by Linda L Franklin.*

4 out of 4 stars

As the word suggests, poems are a mystery a reader is supposed to unravel. And one thing I love about them is the hidden meanings and their preciseness. You never realize when you finish devouring a book full of poems because each has content that transports you to various multiple universes.

Soulful Reflections by Linda L Franklin contains many poems about different thoughts. In one, she reminds us that changes have to occur in life whether we like it or not. Some friends come into our lives then suddenly disappear. Maybe, we once never enjoyed physical exercise. Then we unexpectedly become gym freaks. A formerly curvaceous body changes because of pregnancy hormones. Another poem tells us actions are superior to verbal talks. You cannot say you are my friend yet not show up during my grieving period.

We have a poem about missing a loved one. You miss their touch and caresses. Plus, their smile and humor. Another is about how love is a mutual concession. Partners are supposed to help each other grow, and compromise is part of the process. Linda reminds us that love is full of laughter, forgiveness, passion, and other virtues. Sadness is part of life. The persona remembers a loved one who died and all the plans they had planned to accomplish.

I loved the images the author inserted before each poem. One is of a gigantic tree. Another is of a kangaroo; we have a dolphin, and others I couldn't quite figure out what they were. One particular illustration was a nature trail. I could smell the trees.

I resonated deeply with one poem— "ancestors and me." It describes the heroic work some of our ancestors achieved for us to have a better life. Some came from faraway lands to ensure we had a better life than they did. Our race, religion, and culture primarily depended on them. In the future, we will be ancestors of a generation to come. I loved that.

I did encounter very few errors. As such, *Soulful Reflections* is professionally edited. There was not a sole thing to despise. If anything, the book reminded me of the magnificence and mystery of life. Some people feel like family even though we are not related by blood. I award the work **4 out of 4 stars**. Several poems sounded like songs; I even tried singing them to spice them. As the installment culminated, I found it thrilling how stanzas can cause a whirlpool of emotions: sadness, laughter, stimulation, etc. I recommend it to poem fanatics.

Printed in the United States
by Baker & Taylor Publisher Services